W9-AMA-521

First Facts

Madam C.J. Walker

INVENTOR AND BUSINESSWOMAN

by Lisa M. Bolt Simons

CAPSTONE PRESS
a capstone imprint

First Facts are published by Capstone Press,
1710 Roe Crest Drive, North Mankato, Minnesota 56003
www.mycapstone.com

Library of Congress Cataloging-in-Publication Data:
Library of Congress Cataloging-in-Publication Data is available on the Library of
Congress website.
ISBN: 978-1-5435-0644-0 (library binding) -- 978-1-5435-0650-1 (paperback) --
978-1-5435-0656-3 (ebook)
Summary: Presents the life of Madam C.J. Walker, the businesswoman who was the
first woman to become a self-made millionaire.

Editorial Credits
Anna Butzer, editor; Bobbie Nuytten, designer;
Jo Miller, media researcher; Laura Manthe, production specialist

Photo Credits
A'Lelia Bundles/Madam Walker Family Archives, all images except: Getty Images:
Wallace G. Levison/Contributor, 11; Granger, NYC - All rights reserved., 9

Printed in the United States of America.
010868S18

Table of Contents

CHAPTER 1

Self-Made Millionaire

Madam C.J. Walker built a business around one creation. She made a hair product for African Americans. It helped to grow new hair. It was called "Madam C.J. Walker's Wonderful Hair Grower." After just 12 years of running her business, she became a millionaire.

FACT Madam C.J. Walker was the first woman to become a self-made millionaire.

CHAPTER 2

Escape

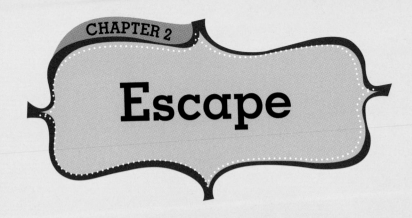

Madam Walker was born on December 23, 1867, in Delta, Louisiana. Her name then was Sarah Breedlove. Her parents were freed slaves. Sarah was born free but lived in **poverty**. She worked in cotton fields. By the age of 7, both of Sarah's parents had died. She then lived with her sister and brother-in-law.

poverty—the state of being poor or without money

Sarah Breedlove lived in a cabin in Delta, Louisiana, until she was 7 years old.

"I know how to grow hair as well as I know how to grow cotton. I have built my own factory on my own ground."

Madam C.J. Walker

Sarah's brother-in-law treated her poorly. She left his home at age 14. She married Moses McWilliams. In 1885 they had a daughter named Lelia. When Sarah was 20 years old, Moses died suddenly. Sarah and Leila moved to St. Louis, Missouri. Sarah worked doing laundry and cooking.

FACT Sarah made $1.50 a day doing laundry.

Women washing laundry

CHAPTER 3

From Suds to Salesperson

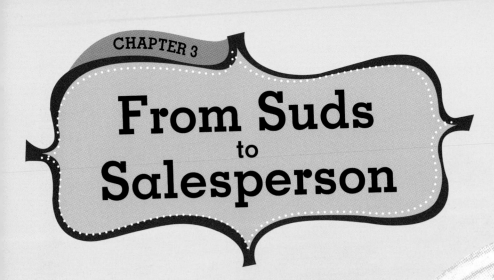

Sarah was barely making enough money. She also was losing her hair. In the early 1900s, Sarah began using "The Great Wonderful Hair Grower." It worked well. Sarah started selling the product for the company's owner, Annie Turnbo, a **chemist**.

chemist—a scientist who studies or works with chemicals

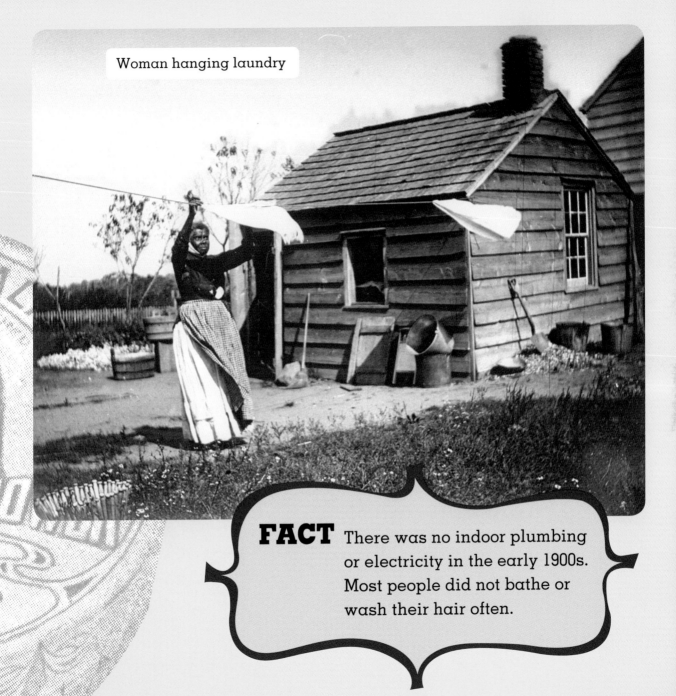

Woman hanging laundry

FACT There was no indoor plumbing or electricity in the early 1900s. Most people did not bathe or wash their hair often.

While in St. Louis, Sarah met Charles Joseph "C.J." Walker. He was a newspaper salesman. In 1905 Sarah and C.J. moved to Denver, Colorado. The next year they married. Sarah changed her name to Madam C.J. Walker. Her daughter became A'Lelia Walker.

"A big black man appeared to me and told me what to mix up for my hair. Some of the remedy was grown in Africa, but I sent for it, put it on my scalp, and in a few weeks my hair was coming in faster than it had ever fallen out."

from Madam C.J. Walker's dream

Madam C.J. Walker in 1915

In 1906 Madam Walker started making her own hair growing product. Her husband helped **advertise** it. Madam Walker sold her Wonderful Hair Grower at churches and in catalogs. She also traveled from house to house. Later her company made other beauty products. Madam Walker wanted her customers to look and feel beautiful. She believed looking beautiful helped her customers live **dignified** lives.

Invest in Yourself

Madam Walker officially formed her business in 1910. She **invested** $10,000 of her own money.

advertise—to give information about something you want to sell

dignified—having or showing honor or respect

invest—to give or lend money to a company

Some of Madam Walker's customers became her sales staff. She trained 40,000 "Walker agents" at hair-**culture** colleges. These agents sold Madam Walker's products in more places. They made money for each product they sold. She helped them get out of poverty. Madam Walker knew what it was like to be poor. She felt proud giving her agents good jobs.

"I am not merely satisfied in making money for myself. I am endeavoring to provide employment for hundreds of women of my race."

Madam C.J. Walker, 1914

culture—a people's way of life, ideas, art, customs, and traditions

Madam Walker driving
her Model T Ford, 1912

CHAPTER 4

The Gift of Giving

Madam Walker did even more for her employees. She encouraged them to stay with her company. She offered money to employees who told others about her **principles**. Madam Walker believed in being open to new ideas. She believed in investing in the future.

FACT Madam Walker improved the hot comb, a styling tool popular in the late 1800s. She made the comb's teeth wider.

principle—a basic law or rule of conduct

A group of Walker agents gather
outside a beautician convention, 1924

"Don't sit down and wait for the
opportunities to come. You have to get
up and make them for yourself!"

Madam C.J. Walker

Madam Walker was also a **philanthropist**. She gave money to **scholarships** and building projects. Later in life Madam Walker struggled with high blood pressure. She died on May 25, 1919, of kidney failure.

"Open your windows—air it well. . . . Keep your teeth clean in order that breath might be sweet. . . . See that your fingernails are kept clean, as that is a mark of refinement."

Madam C.J. Walker in 1915 employee manual,
Hints to Agents

philanthropist—a person who gives time or money to help others

scholarship—money given to a student to help pay for school

Madam Walker
at about the
age of 43

Glossary

advertise (AD-vuhr-tize)—to give information about something you want to sell

chemist (KE-mist)—a scientist who studies or works with chemicals

culture (KUHL-chuhr)—a people's way of life, ideas, art, customs, and traditions

dignified (DIG-nuh-fide)—having or showing honor or respect

invest (in-VEST)—to give or lend money to a company

philanthropist (fuh-LAN-thruh-pist)—a person who gives time or money to help others

poverty (POV-ur-tee)—the state of being poor or without money

principle (PRIN-suh-puhl)—a basic law or rule of conduct

scholarship (SKOL-ur-ship)—money given to a student to help pay for school

Read More

Carson, Mary Kay. *Who Was the Hair-Care Millionaire? Madam C.J. Walker*. New York: Enslow Publishers, 2012.

McAneney, Caitie. *Madam C.J. Walker and Her Beauty Empire*. New York: Rosen Publishing Group, 2016.

McKissack, Patricia and Frederick. *Madam C.J. Walker: Inventor and Millionaire*. New York: Enslow Publishers, 2013.

Internet Sites

Use FactHound to find Internet sites related to this book.

Visit *www.facthound.com*

Just type in 9781543506440 and go!

Check out projects, games and lots more at
www.capstonekids.com

Critical Thinking Questions

1. What are some things Madam C.J. Walker did in her life to help make her successful?

2. How does the quote on page 16 relate to the main text on that page?

3. Why do you think Madam C.J. Walker wanted to empower African Americans?

Index